THE RIVER DREAM

I0834541

THE RIVER DREAM

by
Laurence David

Photographs by
Cathy David
Laurence David
Carol Maras

RESOURCE *Publications* • Eugene, Oregon

THE RIVER DREAM

Copyright © 2016 Laurence David. All rights reserved. Except for brief quotations in critical publications or reviews, no part of this book may be reproduced in any manner without prior written permission from the publisher. Write: Permissions, Wipf and Stock Publishers, 199 W. 8th Ave., Suite 3, Eugene, OR 97401.

Resource Publications
An Imprint of Wipf and Stock Publishers
199 W. 8th Ave., Suite 3
Eugene, OR 97401

www.wipfandstock.com

PAPERBACK ISBN: 978-1-4982-9718-9
HARDCOVER ISBN: 978-1-4982-9720-2
EBOOK ISBN: 978-1-4982-9719-6

Manufactured in the U.S.A. 07/15/16

Only the sun can envision

that bright future on the horizon.

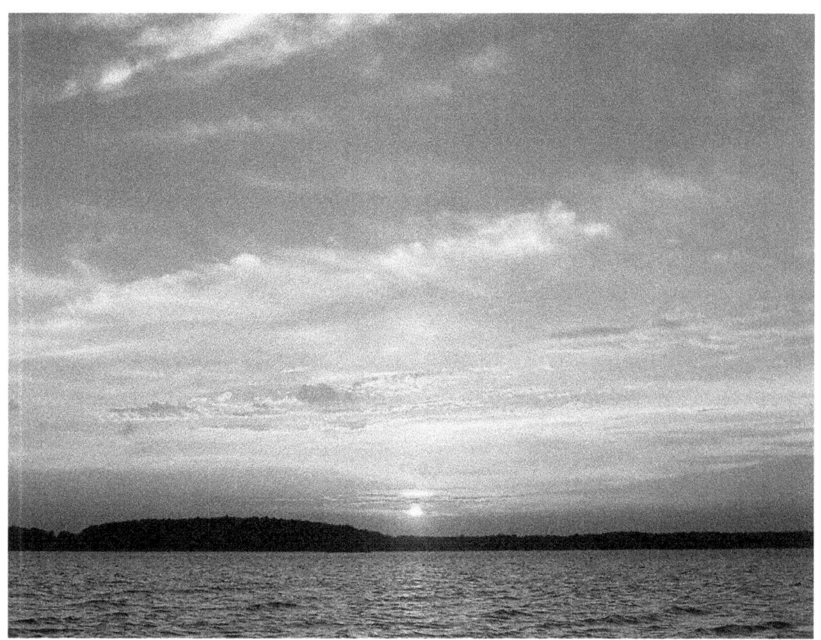

The mystery of creation is not knowing

what form its spirit will take.

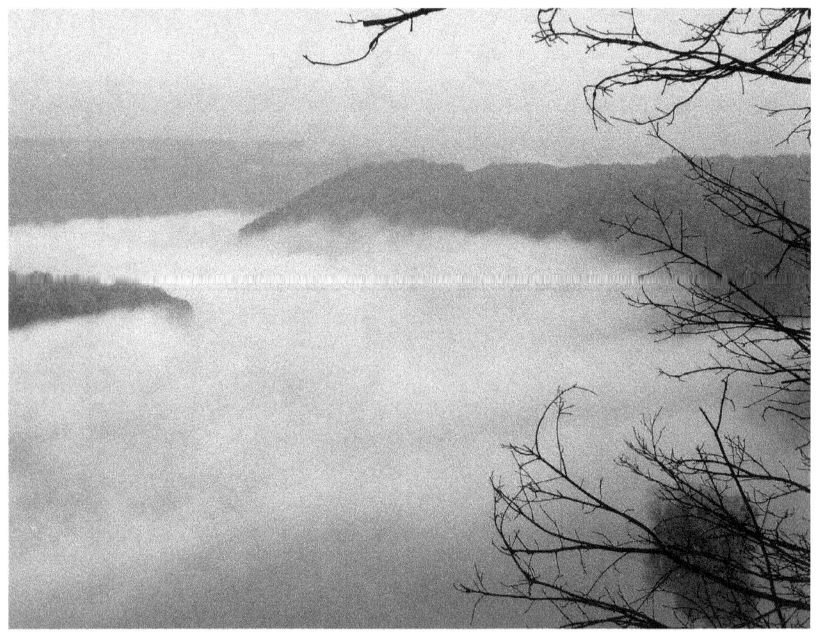

Nature possesses the hope

that what God has created will praise Him.

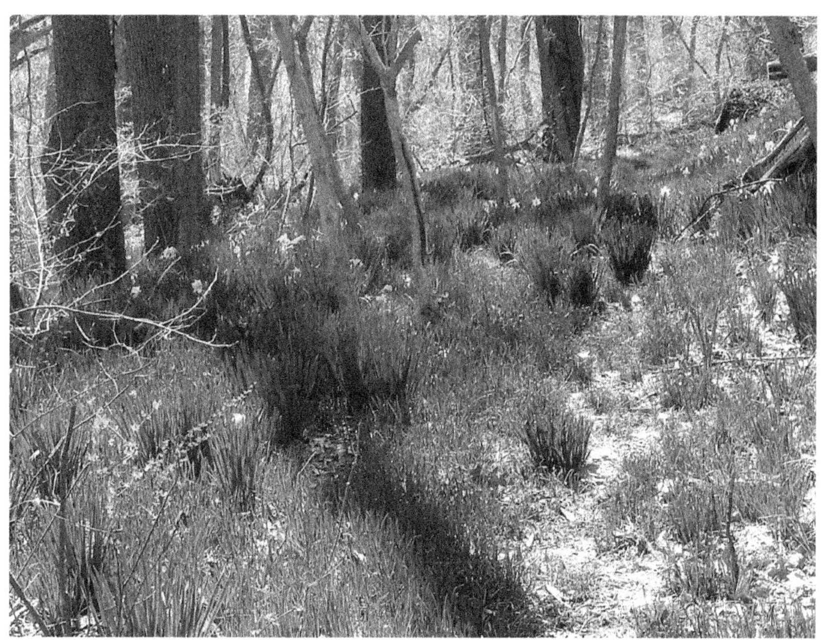

With faith there's still a chance

for the possibility of hope.

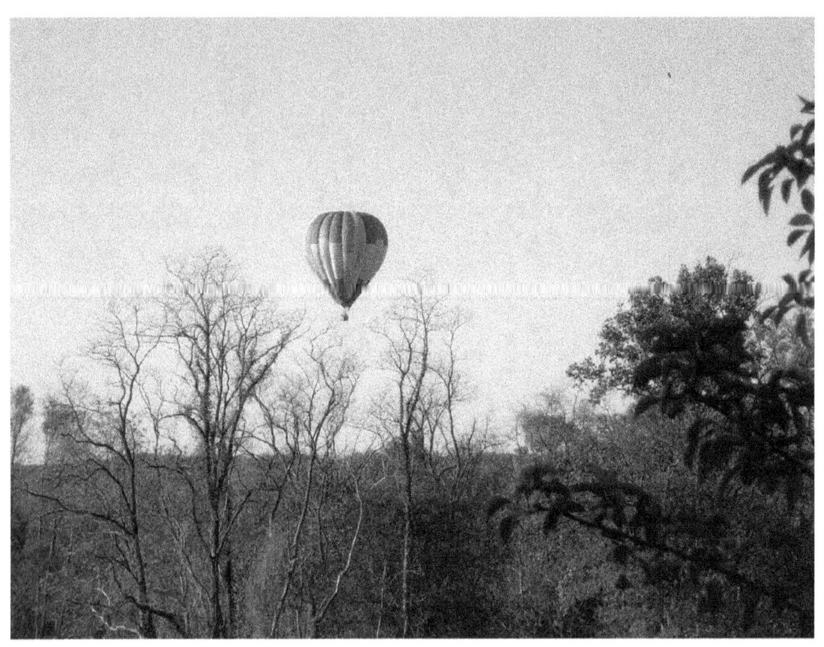

Like the wind, the Spirit drifts along,

waiting for someone to come.

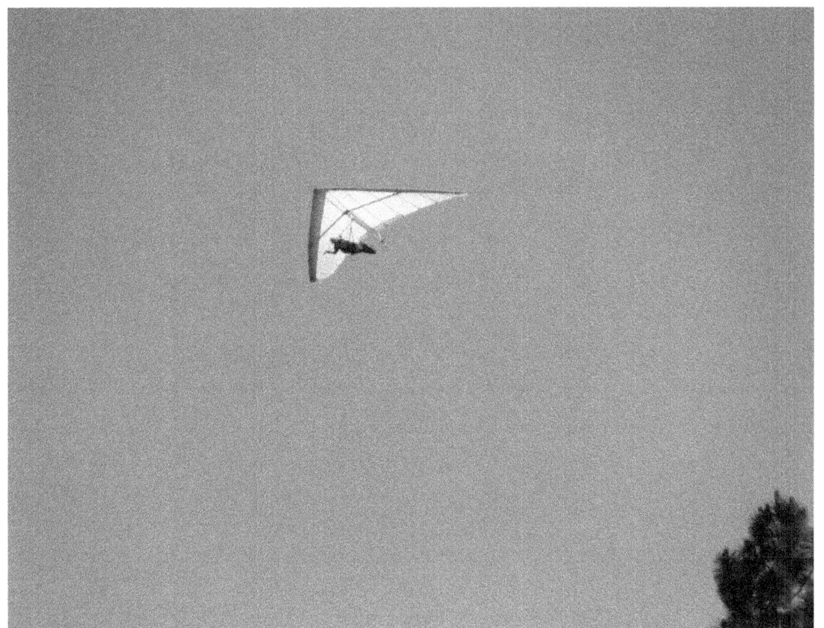

A light that is truly visionary

can see its way out of obscurity.

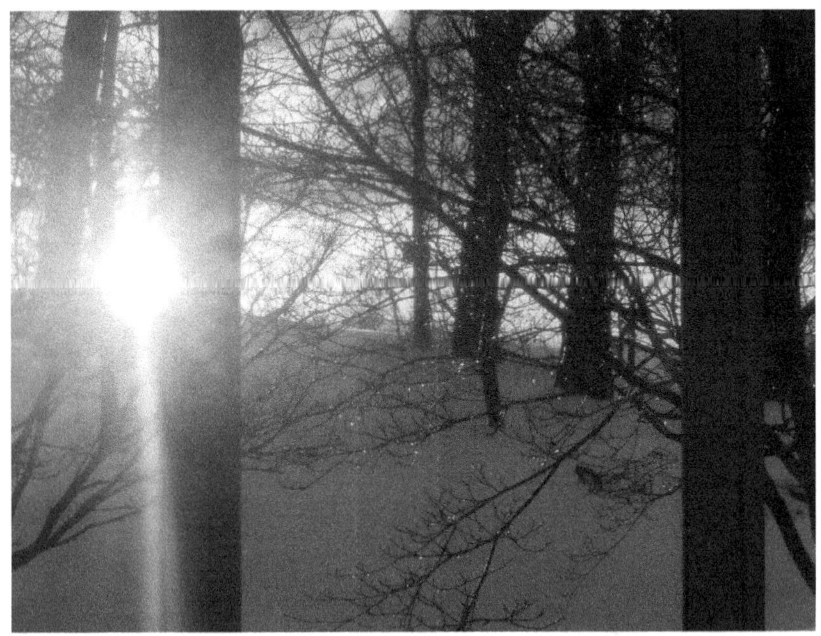

A wise man watches the world go by

and sees the hidden miracles of life behind it.

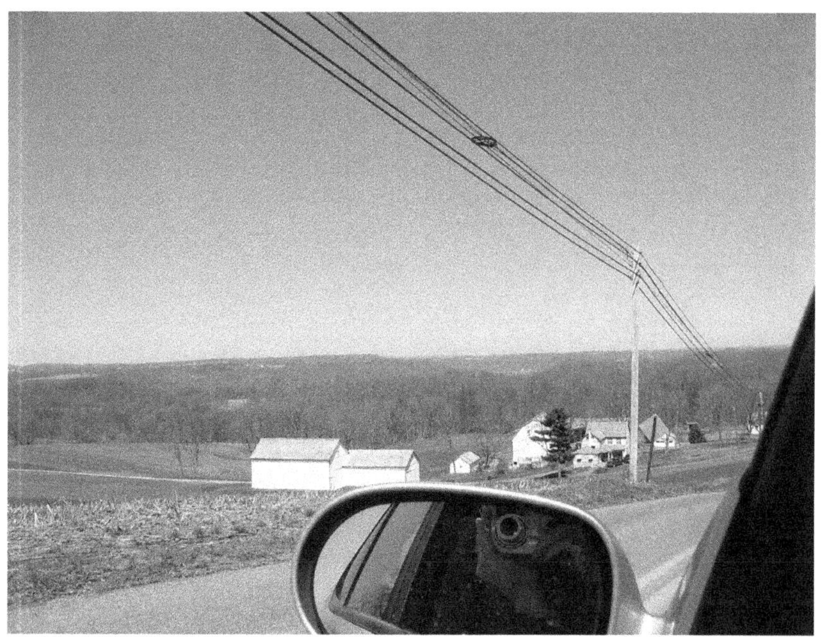

You can't hold the hand that's closed

or ever own the open road.

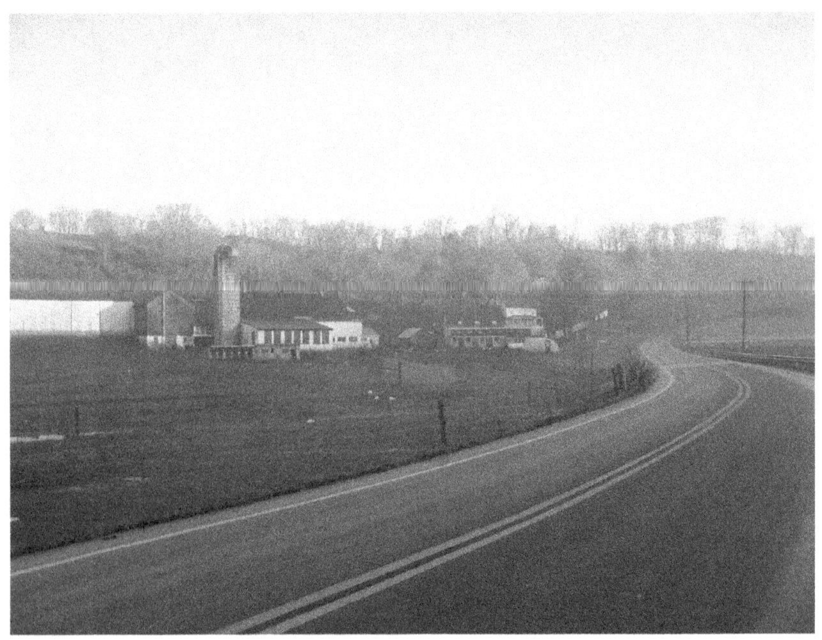

What a new direction may hold

is an old familiar road.

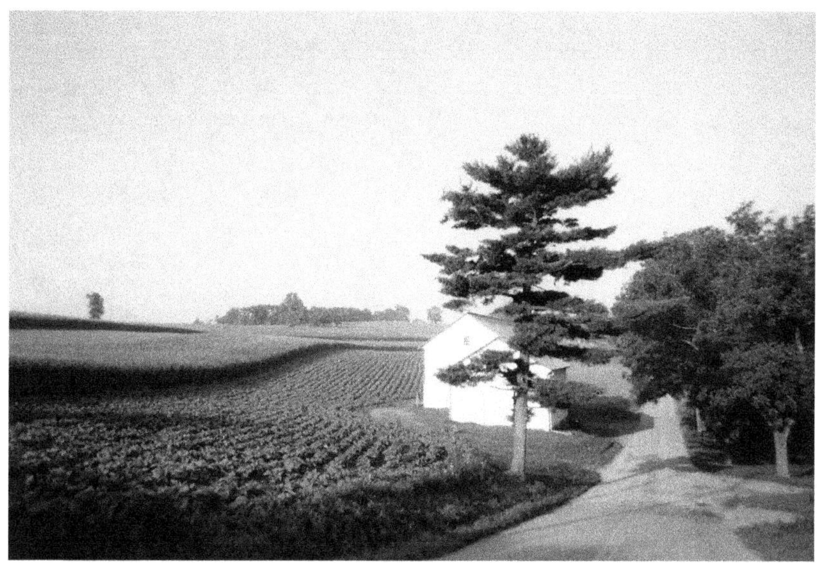

Leave it to the rider

to put pressure on the wheel.

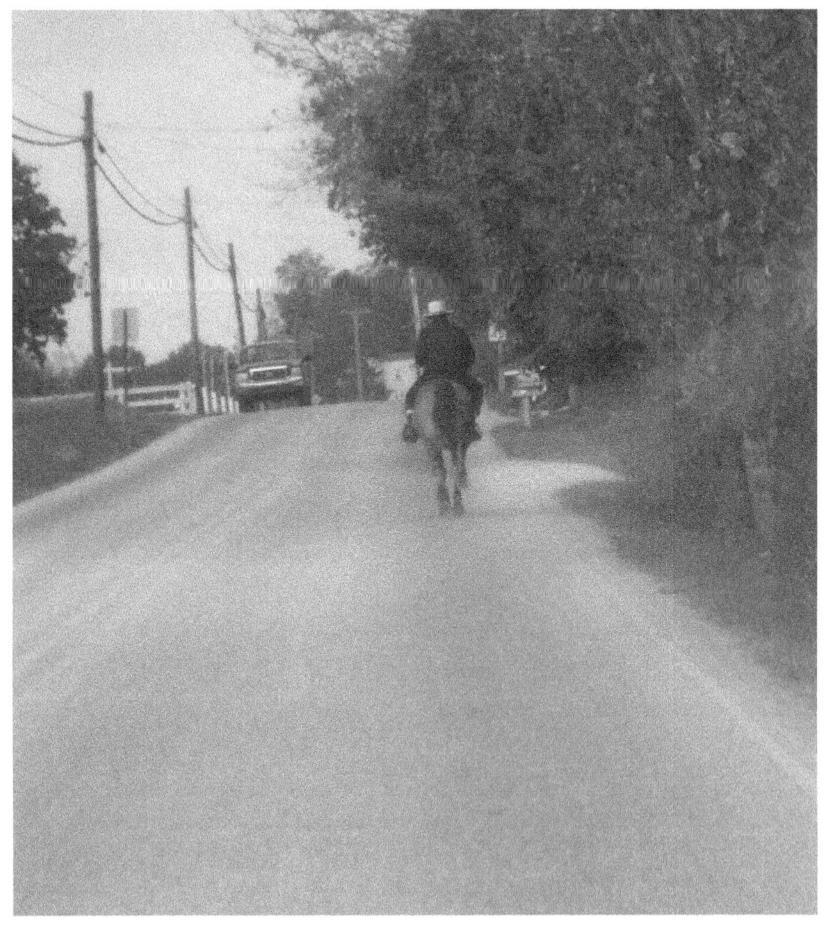

Take one step out of line

and you will surely trip up the rhyme.

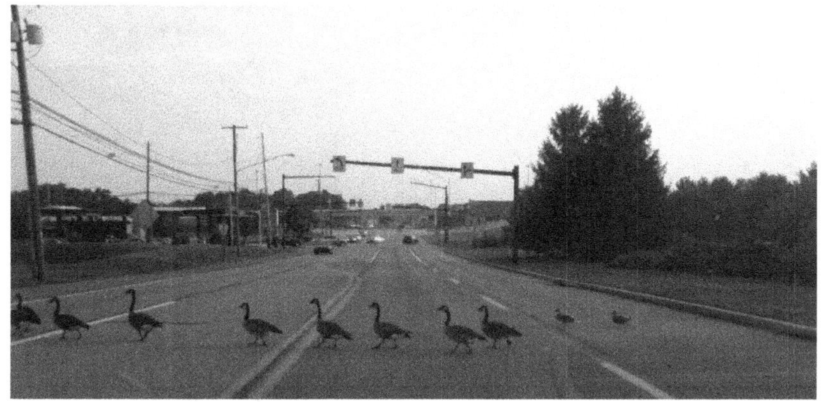

All but one path reaches the door,

falling one step short.

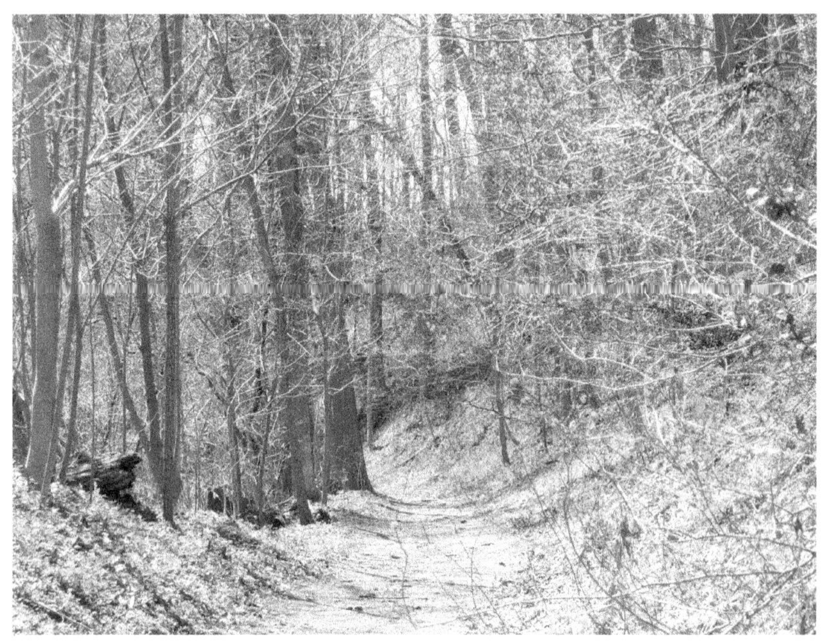

It's only a small leap

from seed to fallen leaf.

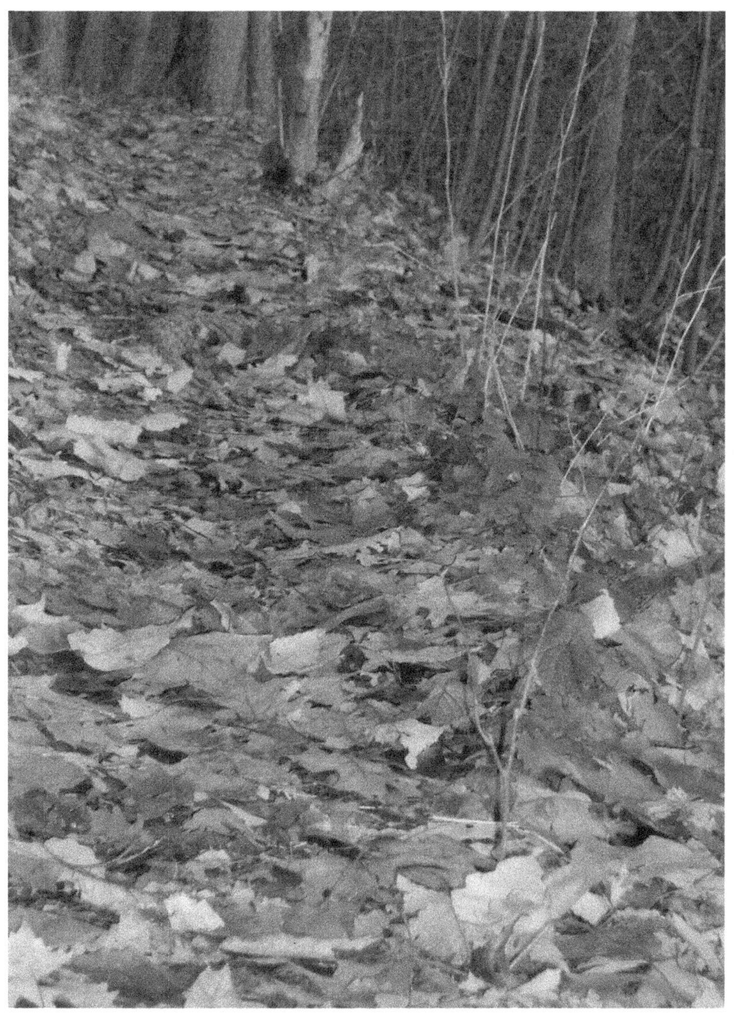

A leap of faith is your best chance
from either side of the fence.

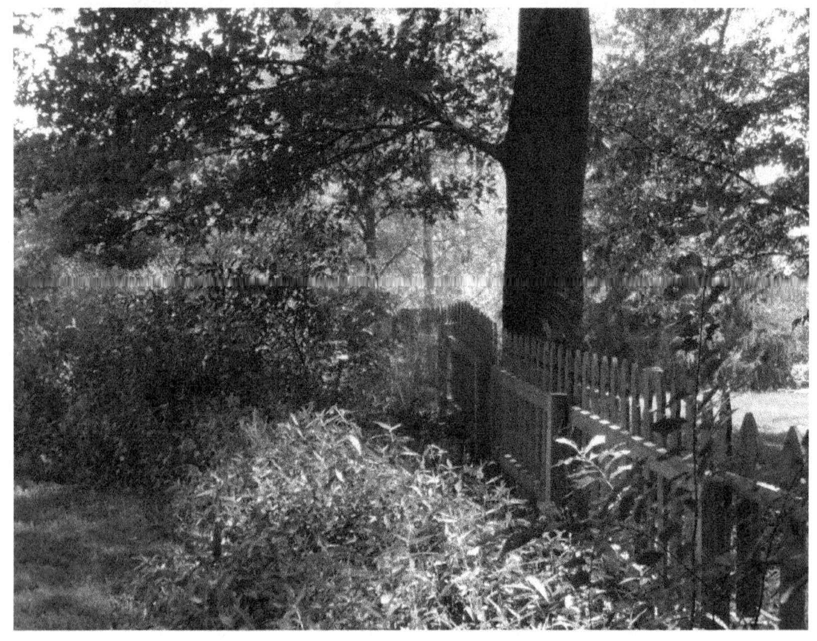

The tiny steps leading up to a high place

is a waterfall bringing us back down to earth.

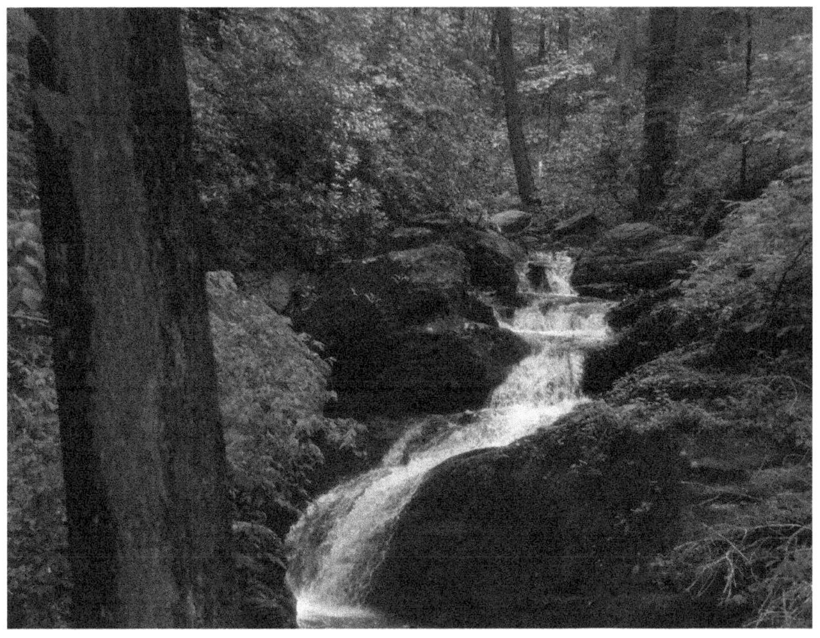

A river prayer spills over

into a warm embrace.

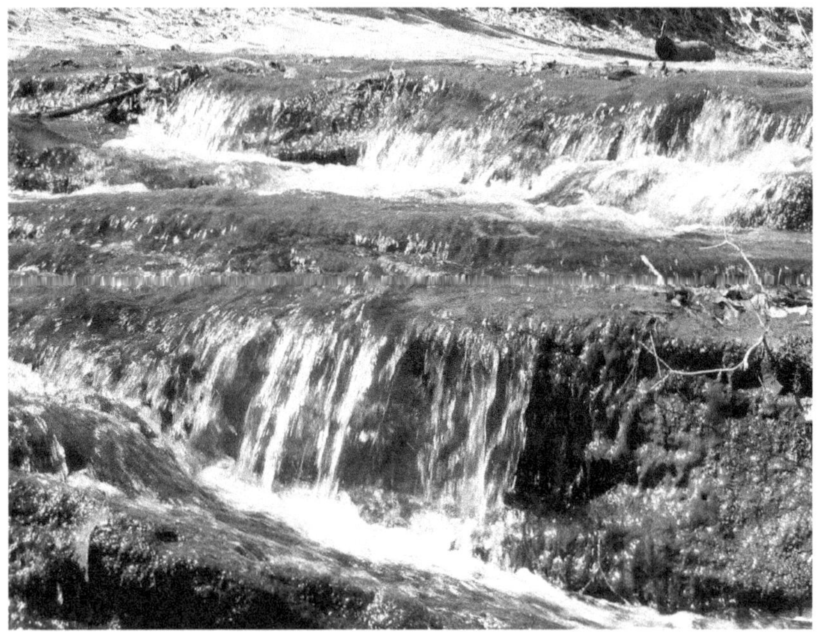

Ride out each new current

until all the ripples settle.

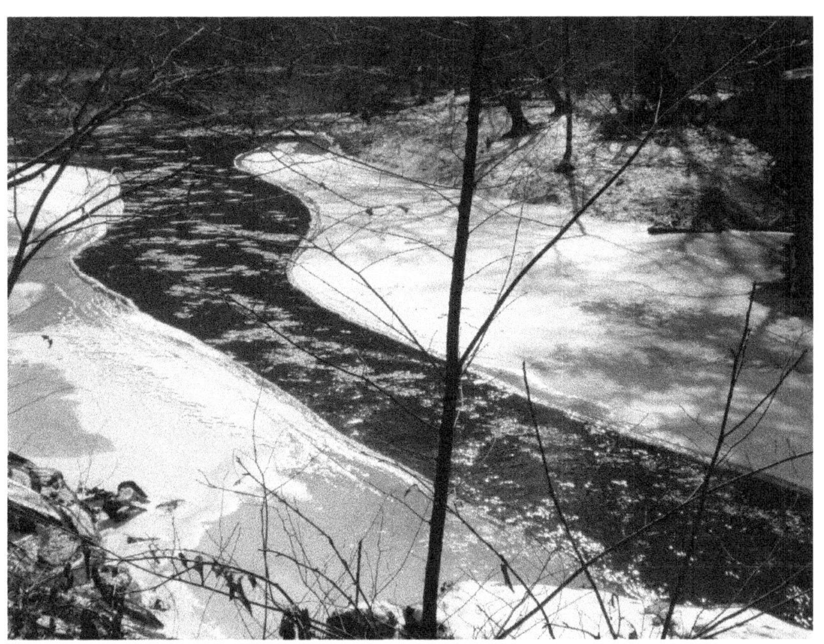

It’s a false sense of peace

that draws you into those dark waters.

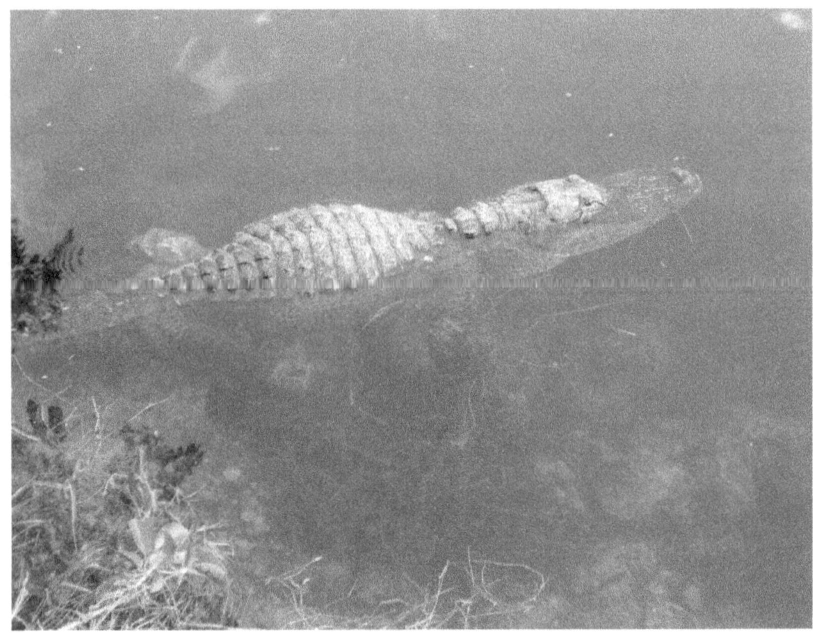

The power of darkness

crawls deep into the night.

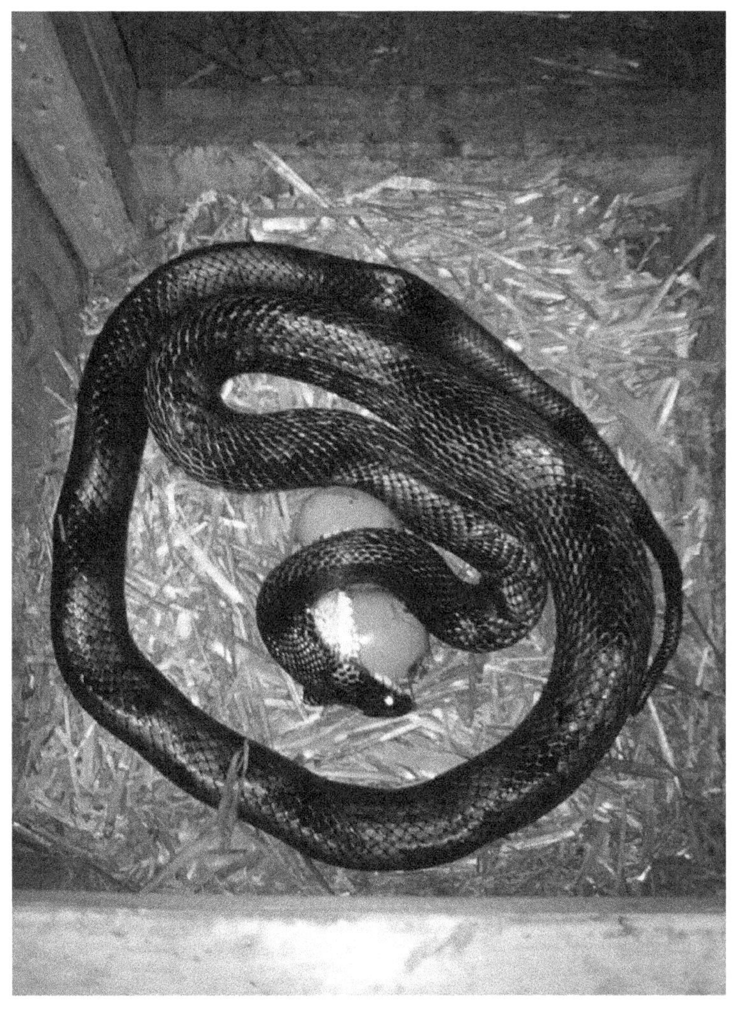

Spreading the worst kind of venom

is the tongue whose words are poison.

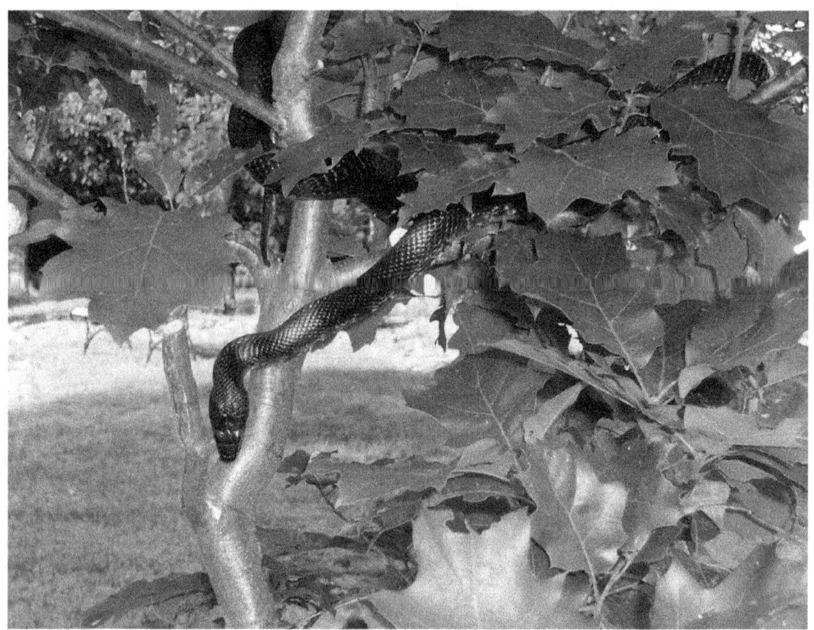

The cruel heart of nature

can be as meticulous as a spider.

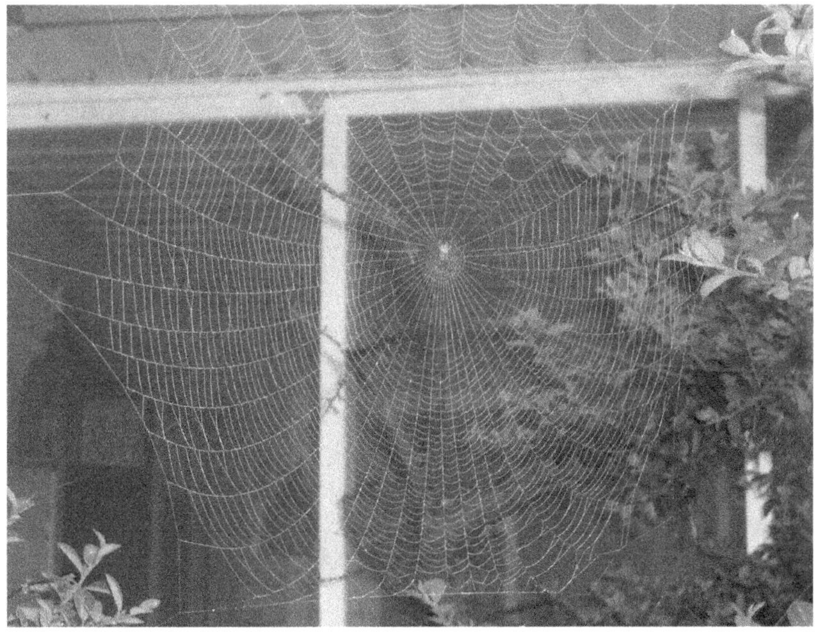

By traveling back in prayer

you will crack the hidden barrier.

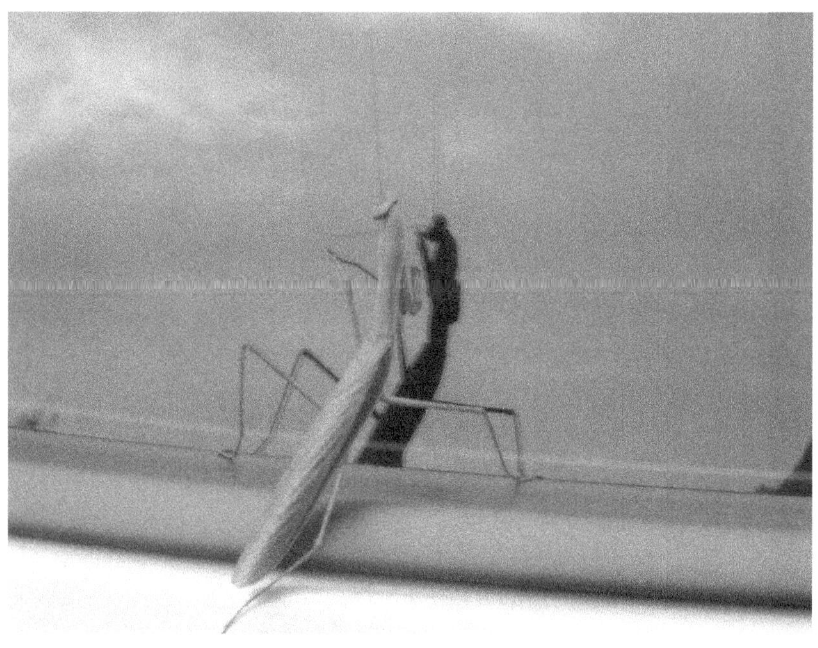

The honey bee's sweet deceit:

the sweetest honey beyond our reach.

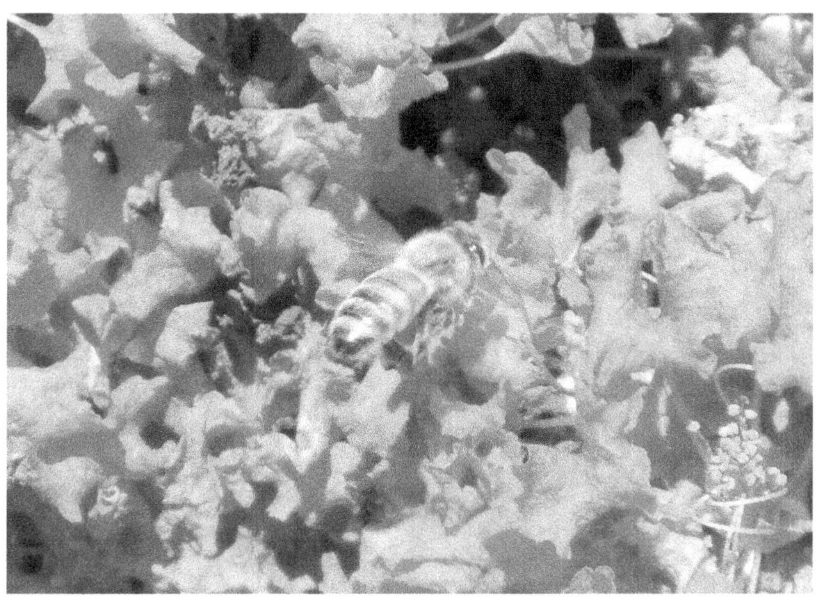

After the sting of one bee,

you count them all as the enemy.

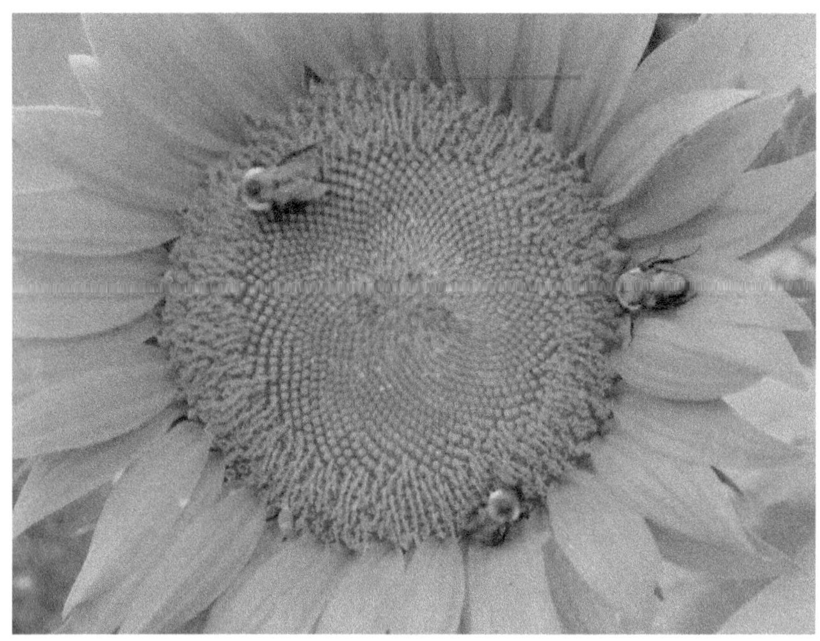

To capture the Spirit in your hands
takes all the strength restraint demands.

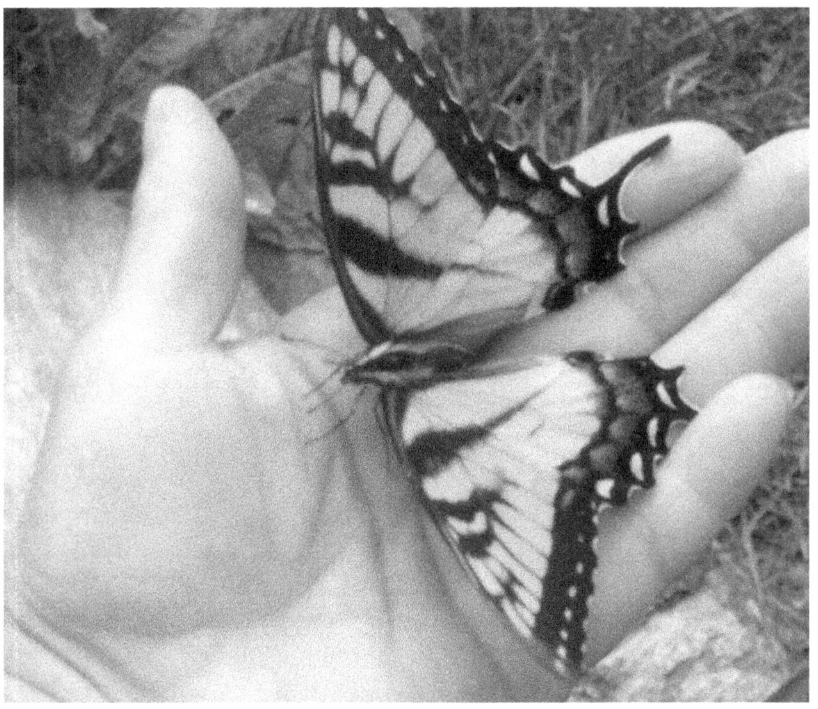

A shattered dream

is like a broken wing.

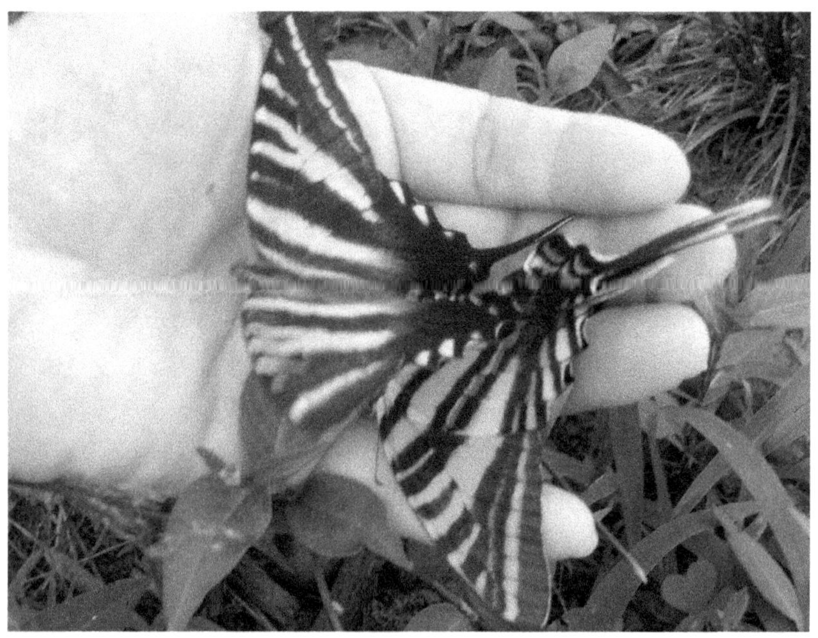

Time that flies between past and present
only rests in the spirit of the moment.

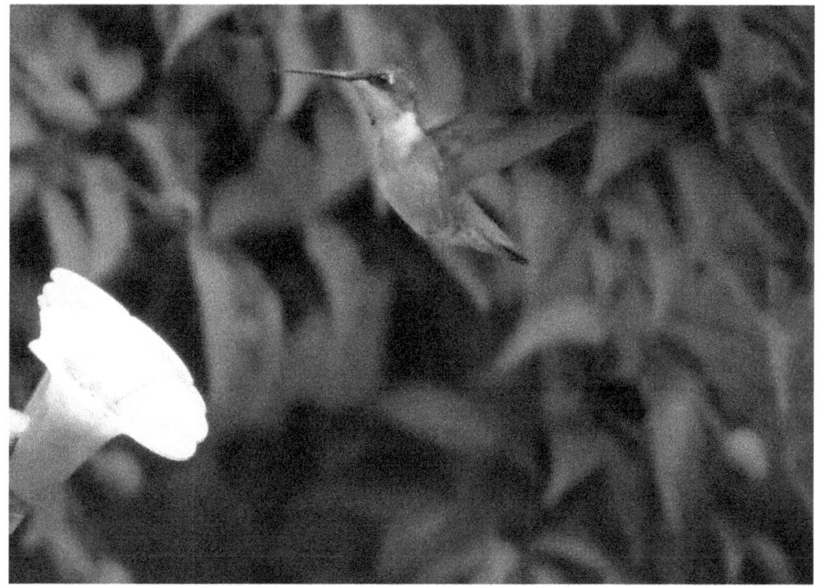

A well deserved reward

should be forever savored.

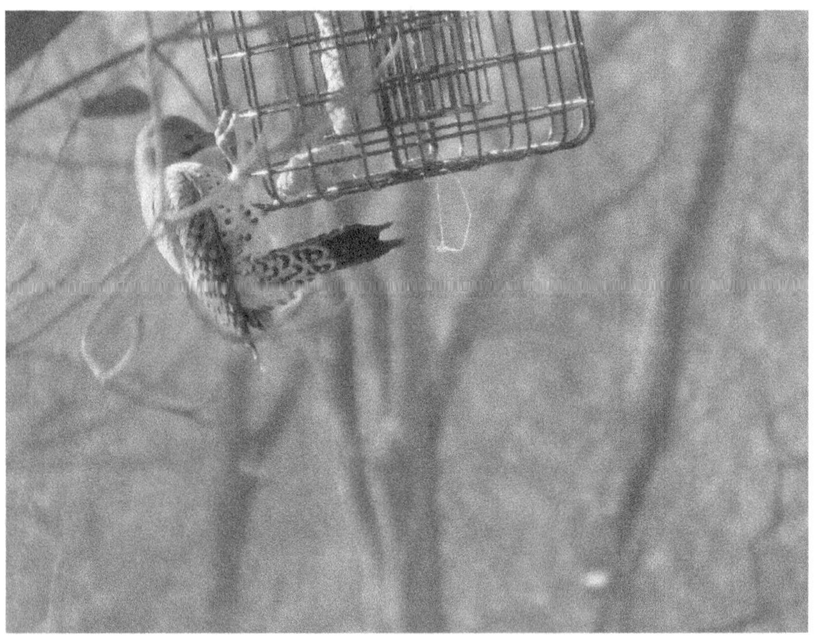

That two come from one is the law of separation:

that two become one is the law of restoration.

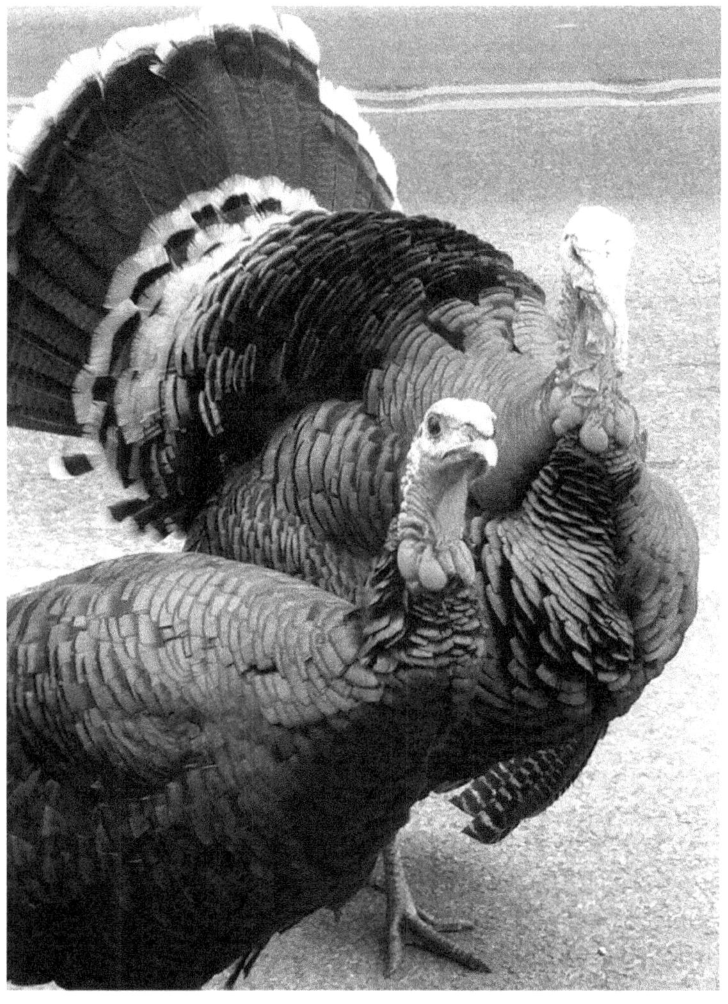

Sometimes our love is like a flower we see from a distance turning in the wind, thinking it to be a bird about to fly.

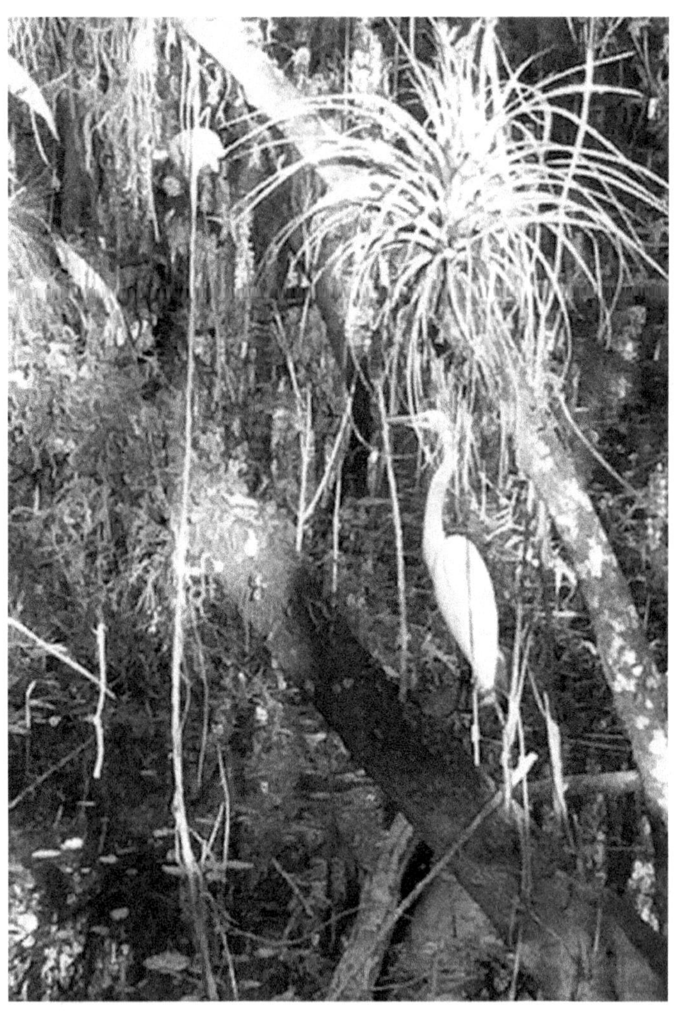

The rose half-opened

hides the strongest scent.

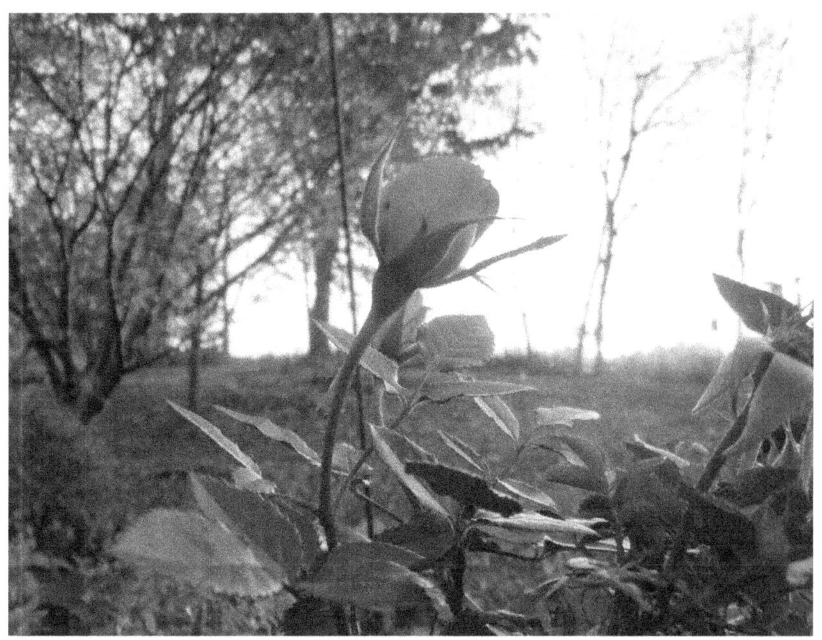

What can freeze you to the bone

can also burn through to your soul.

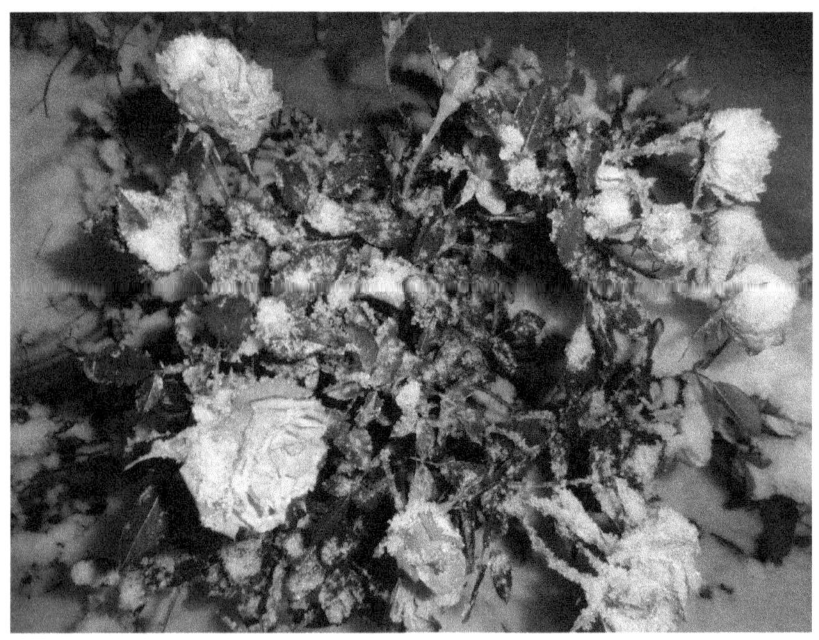

If it's in God's plan

every thread is interwoven.

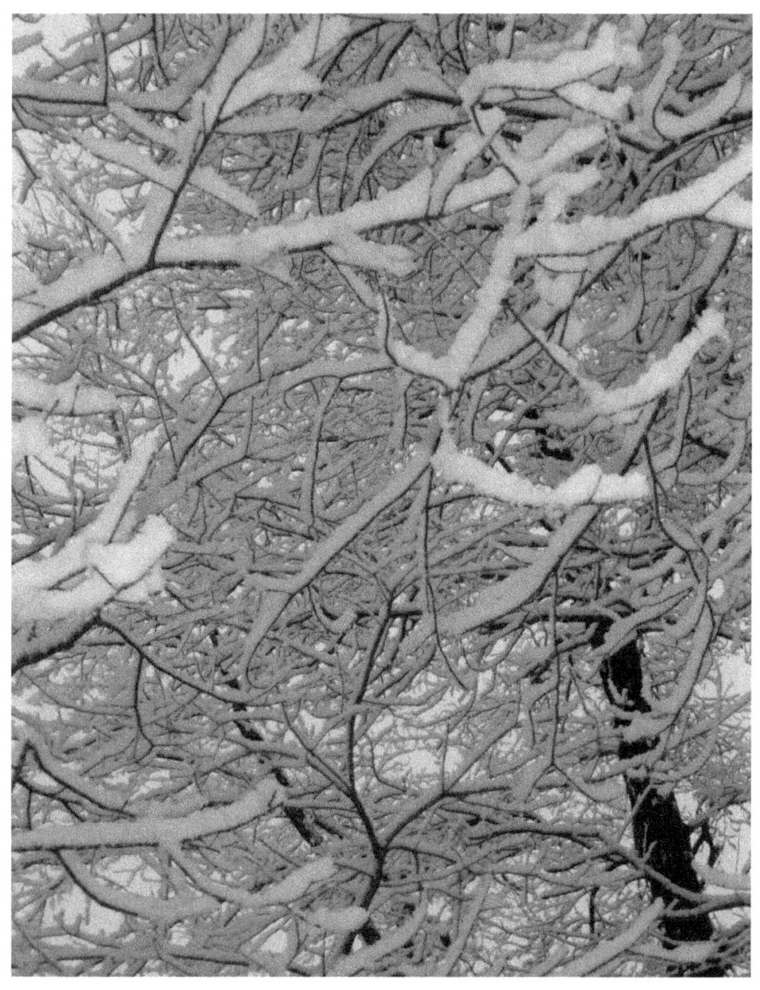

The true Mystery is too simple

for the mind to unravel.

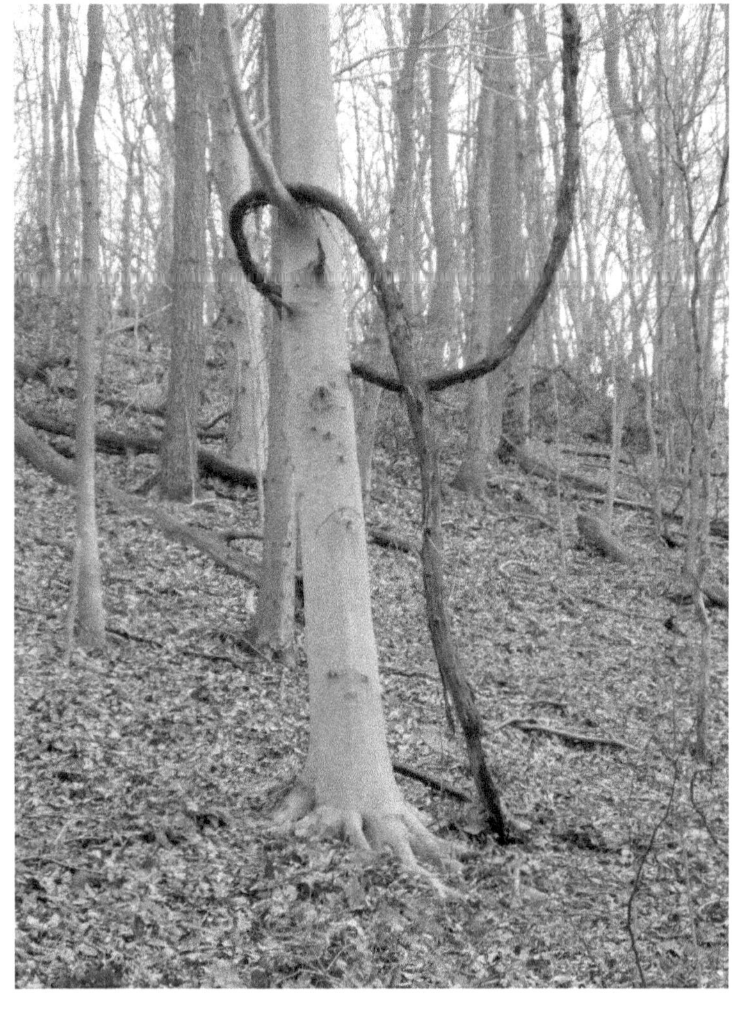

Seize the divine moment

that goes beyond time and space.

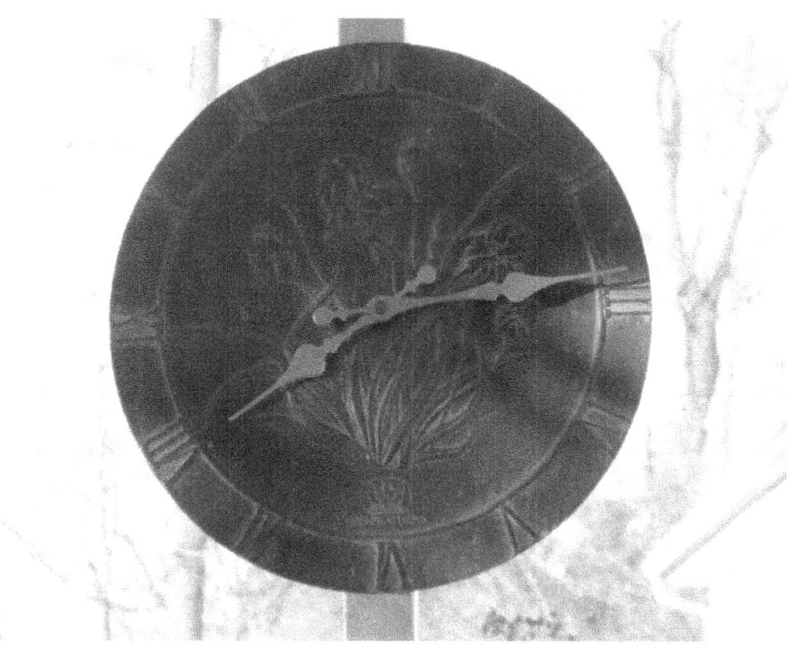

Leave a door open to remind you

not to burn any bridges behind you.

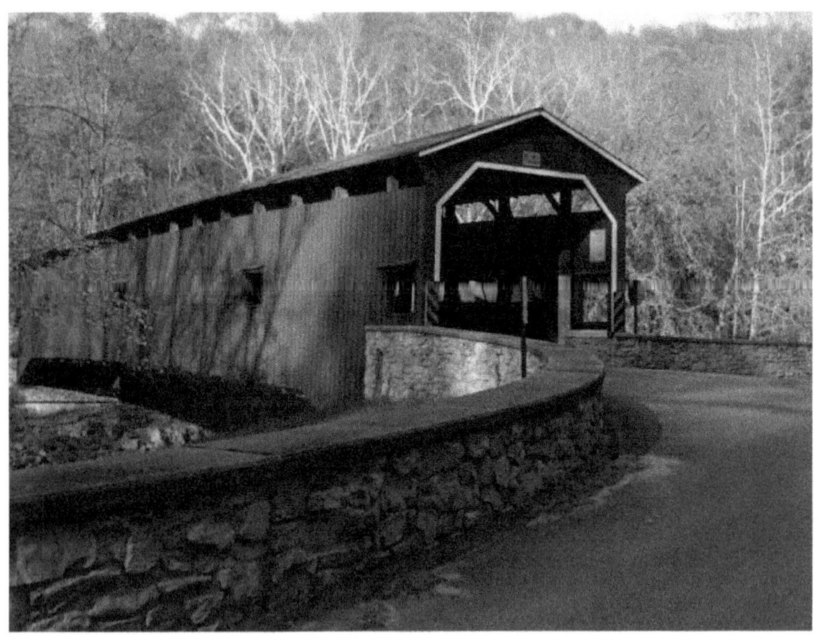

The place that death visits

is left behind in silence.

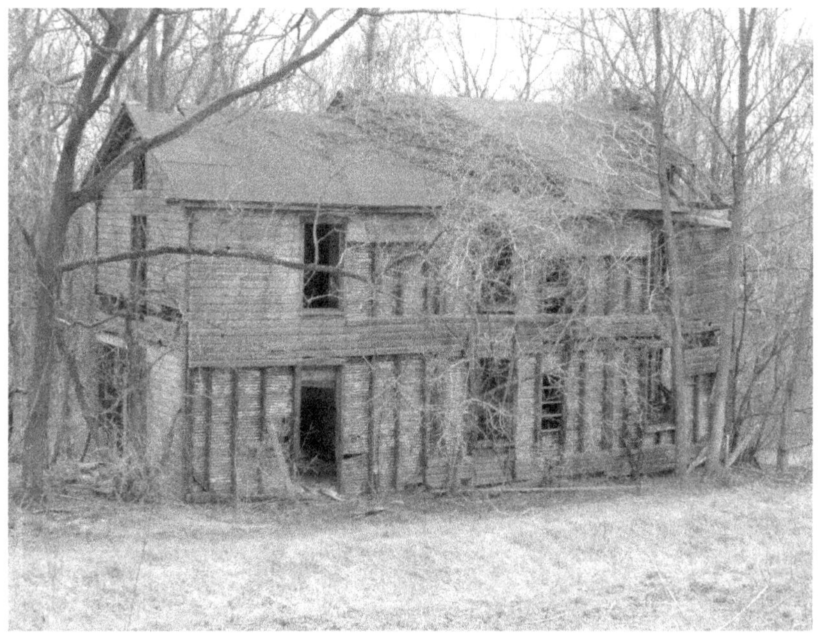

Before death could be defeated

a Tree of Life was uprooted.

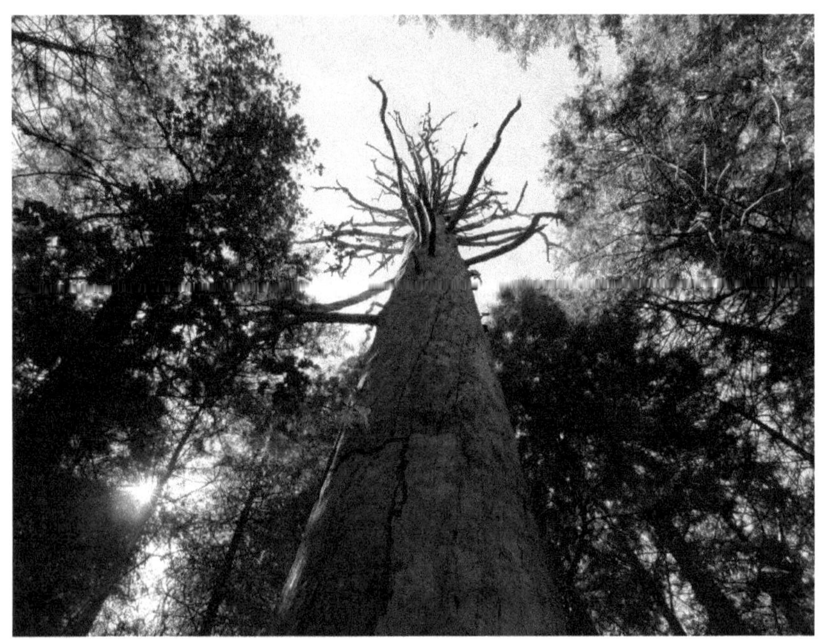

That Light is somehow blessed

which shines from this darkness.

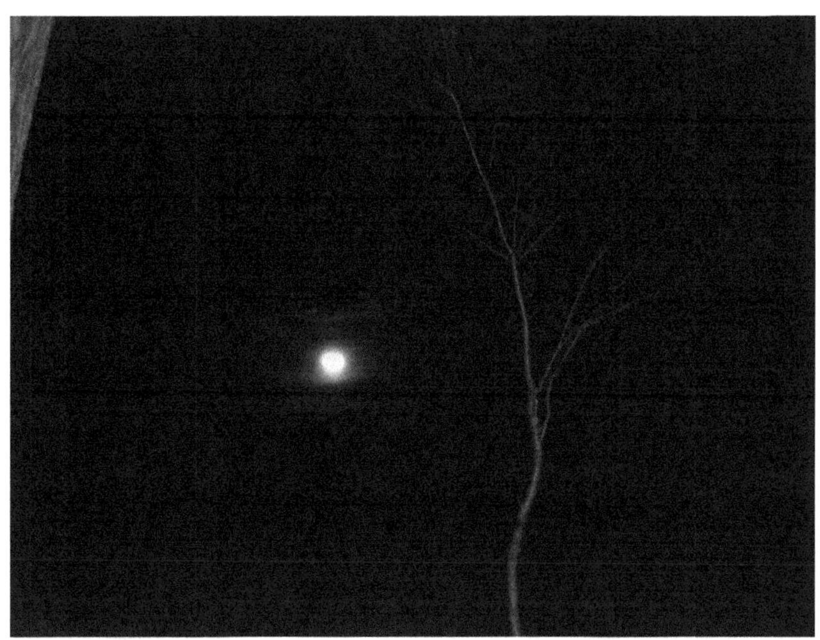

Against the call to arms

is no resistance to peace.

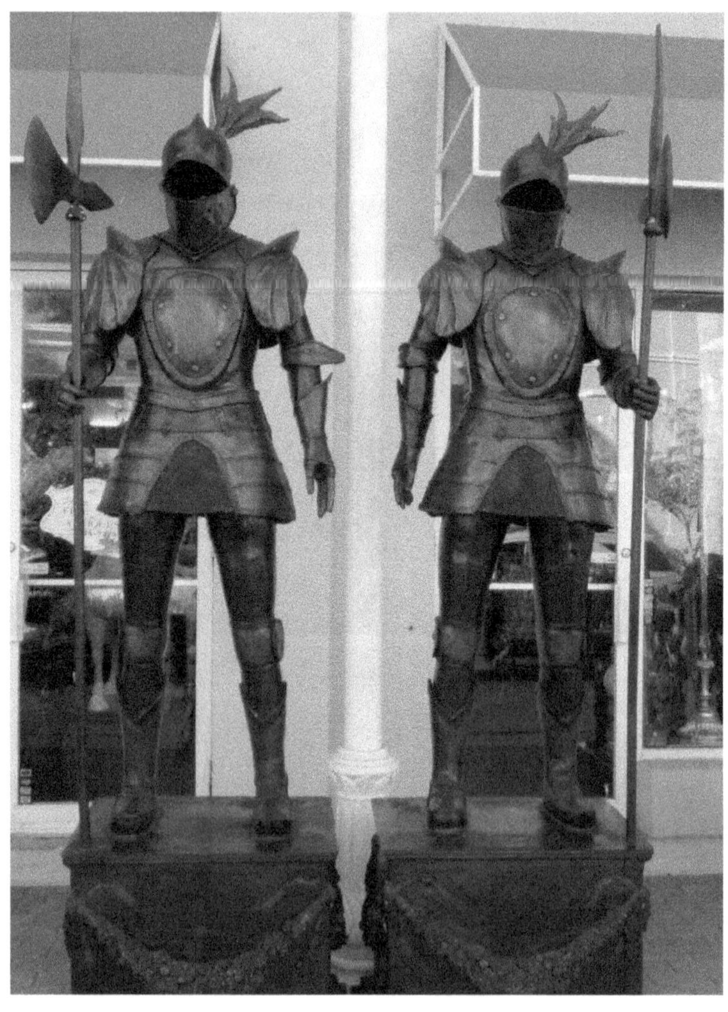

Let your anger be the fire

that disperses like smoke.

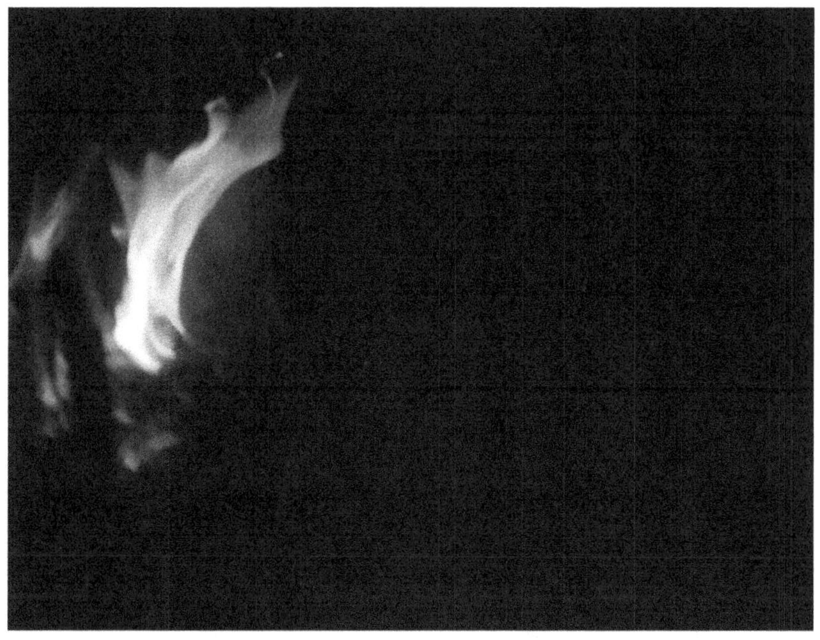

Pride stands before the mountain,

not knowing it will fall.

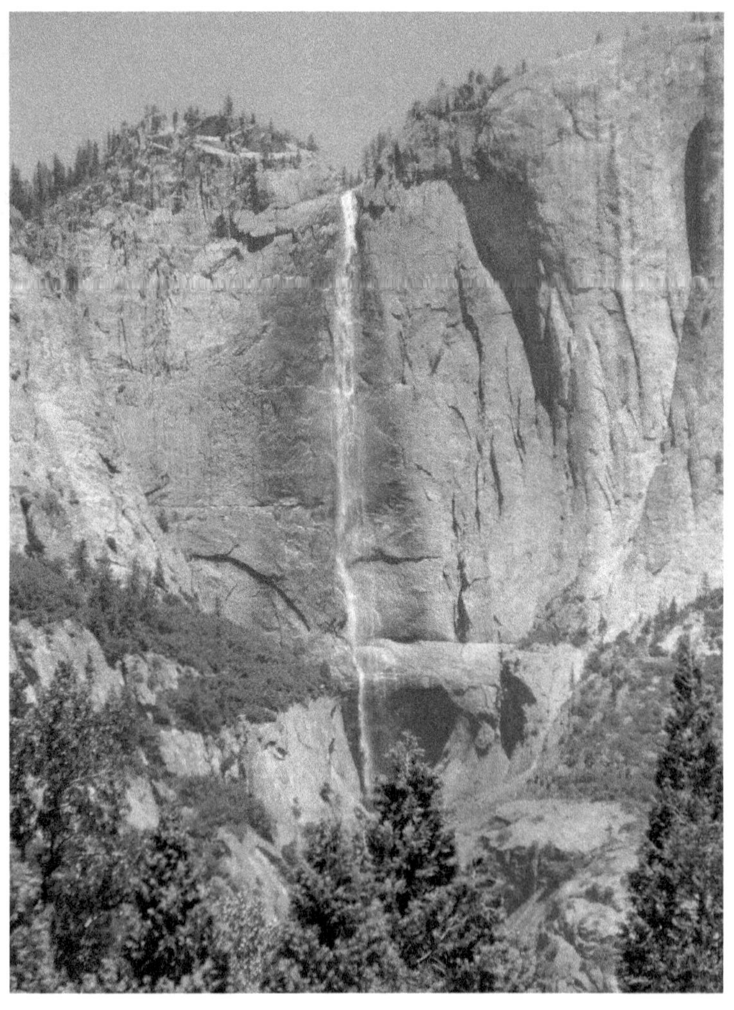

The visionary man sees the

symbolic Christ in the natural world.

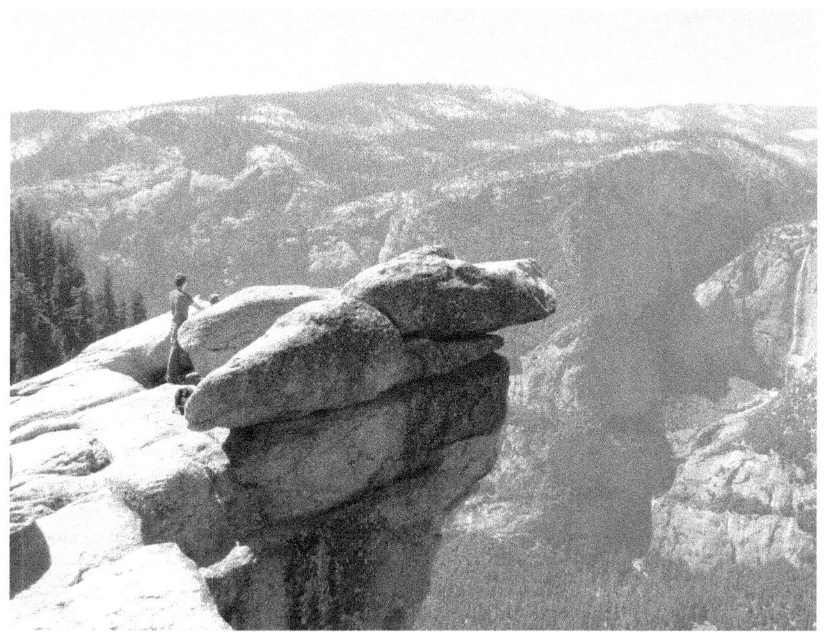

The only doctrine of the Spirit

is to be a child and believe.

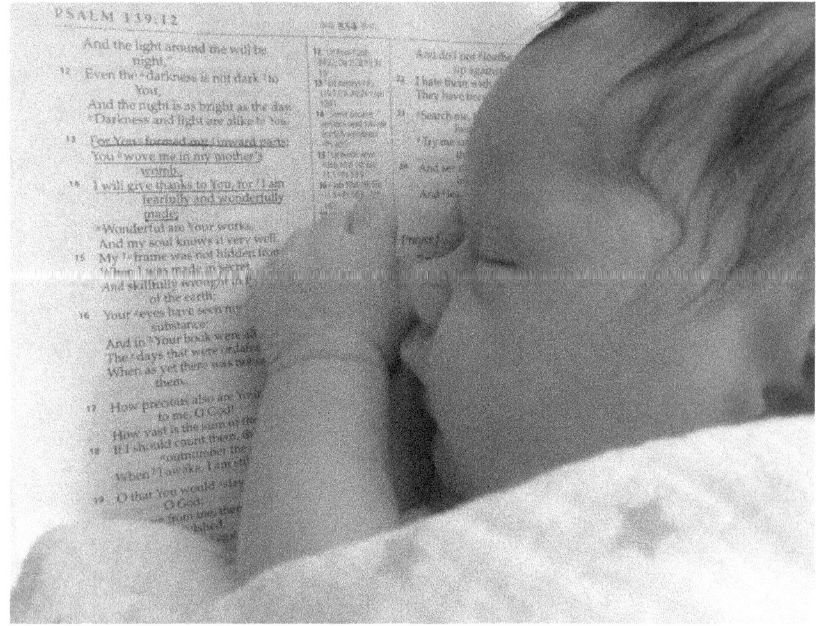

From the Father above

comes true Mother Love.

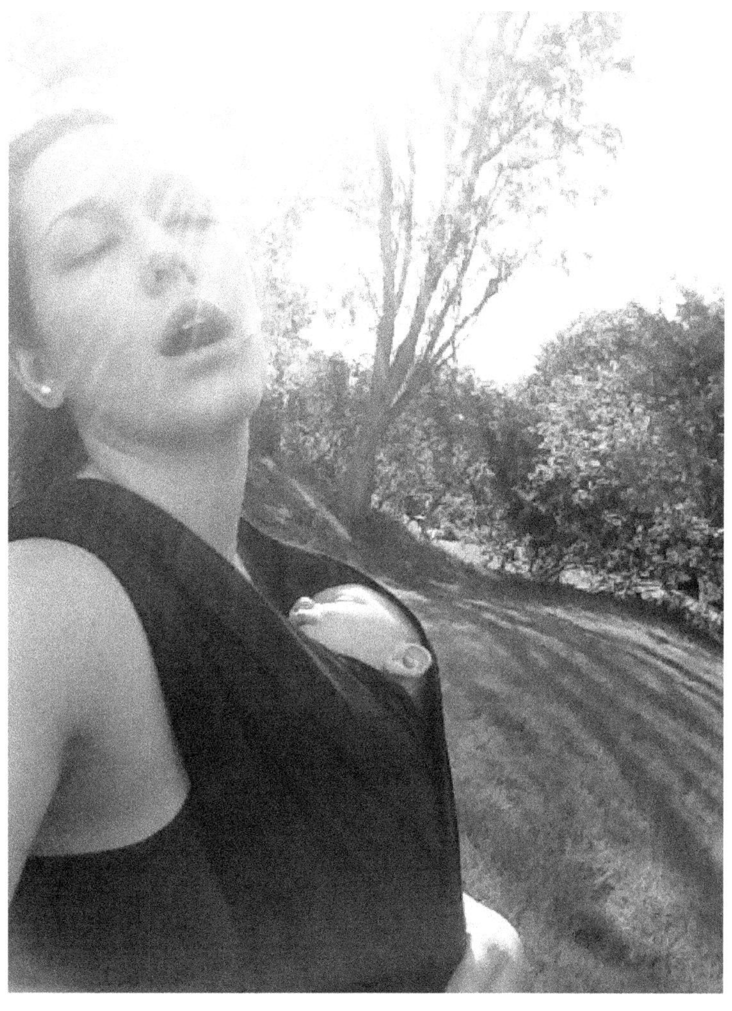

There's no shame in playing the fool

for a heart that's true.

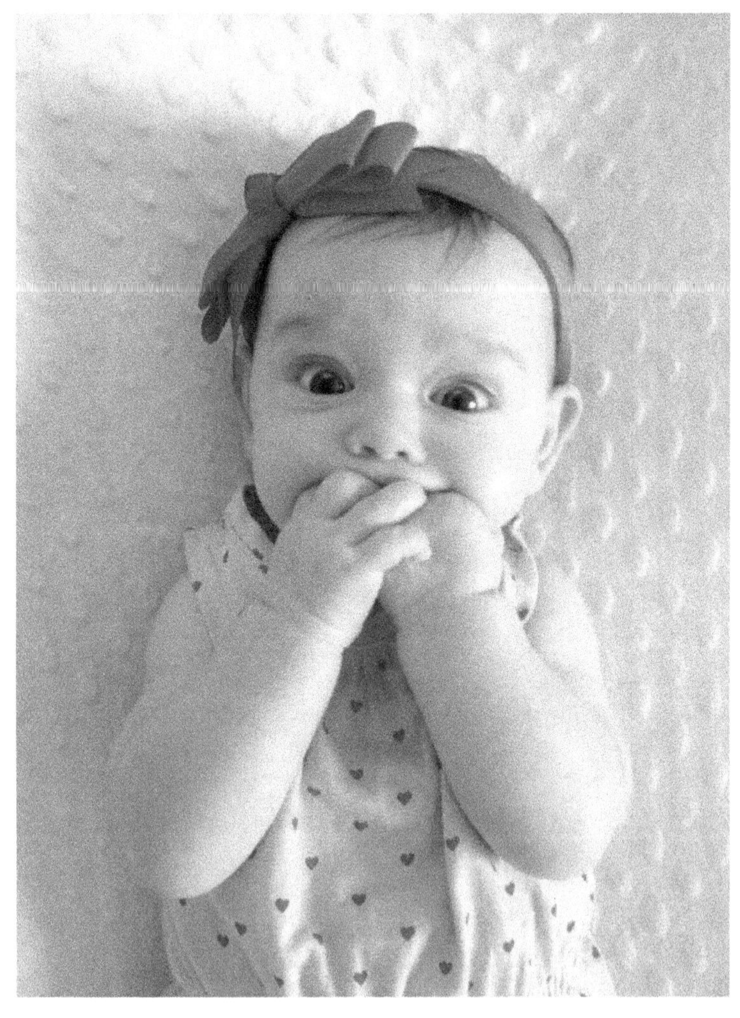

When it concerns love,

you must play the child and the fool.

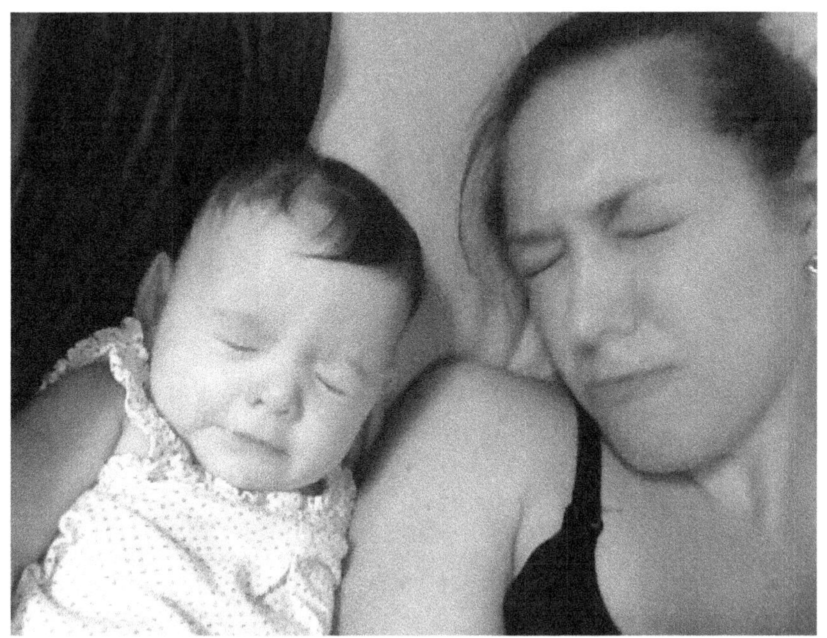

Love is an ocean, but we

must drink from the fountain.

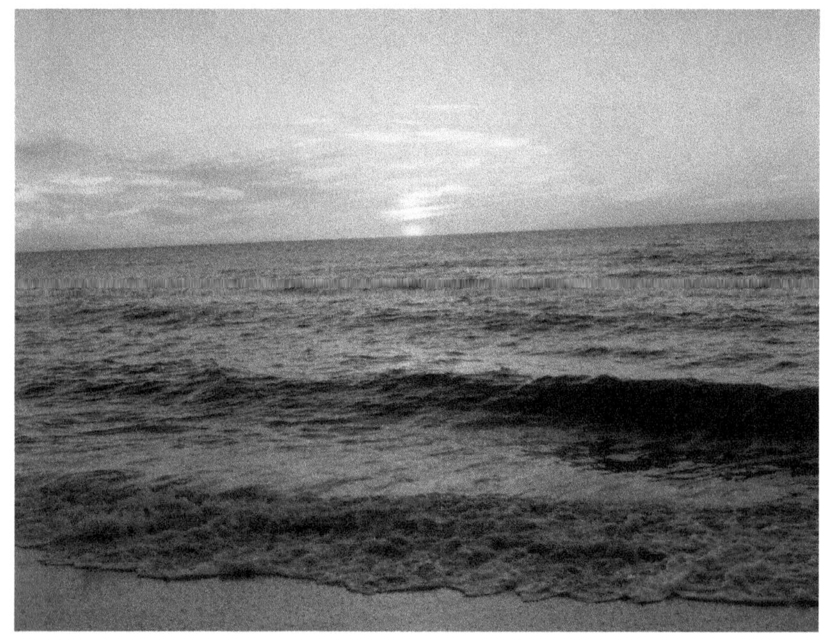

A pearl is found

in the heart of a shell.

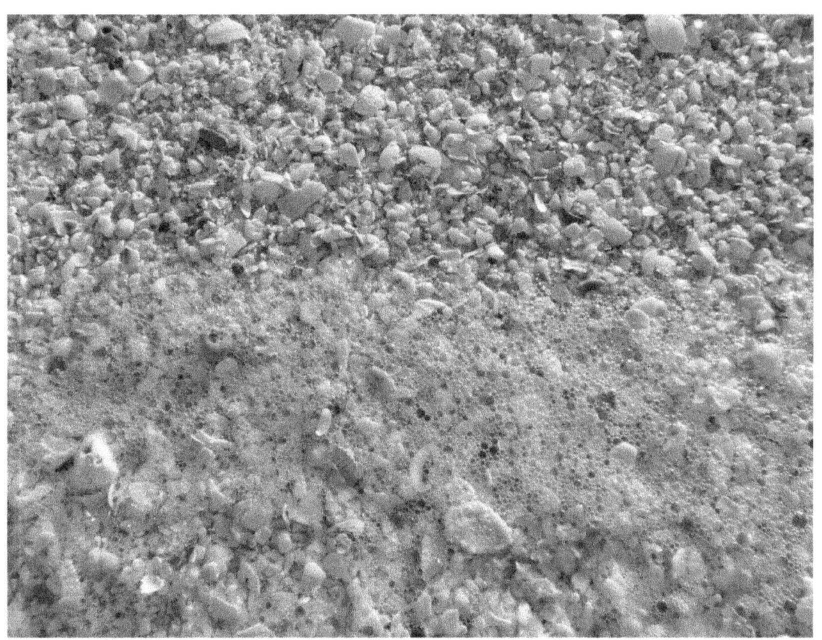

A river calls you home

when your spirit settles in to calm.

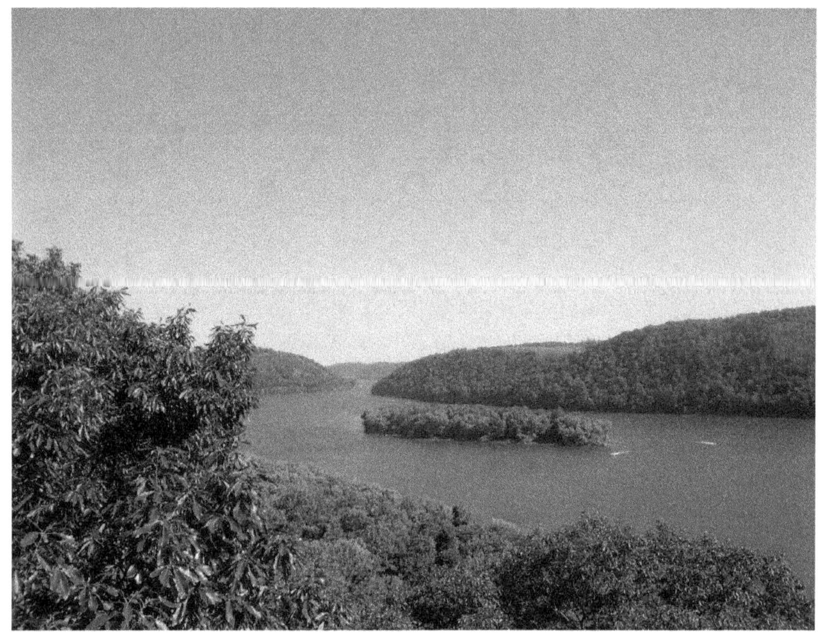

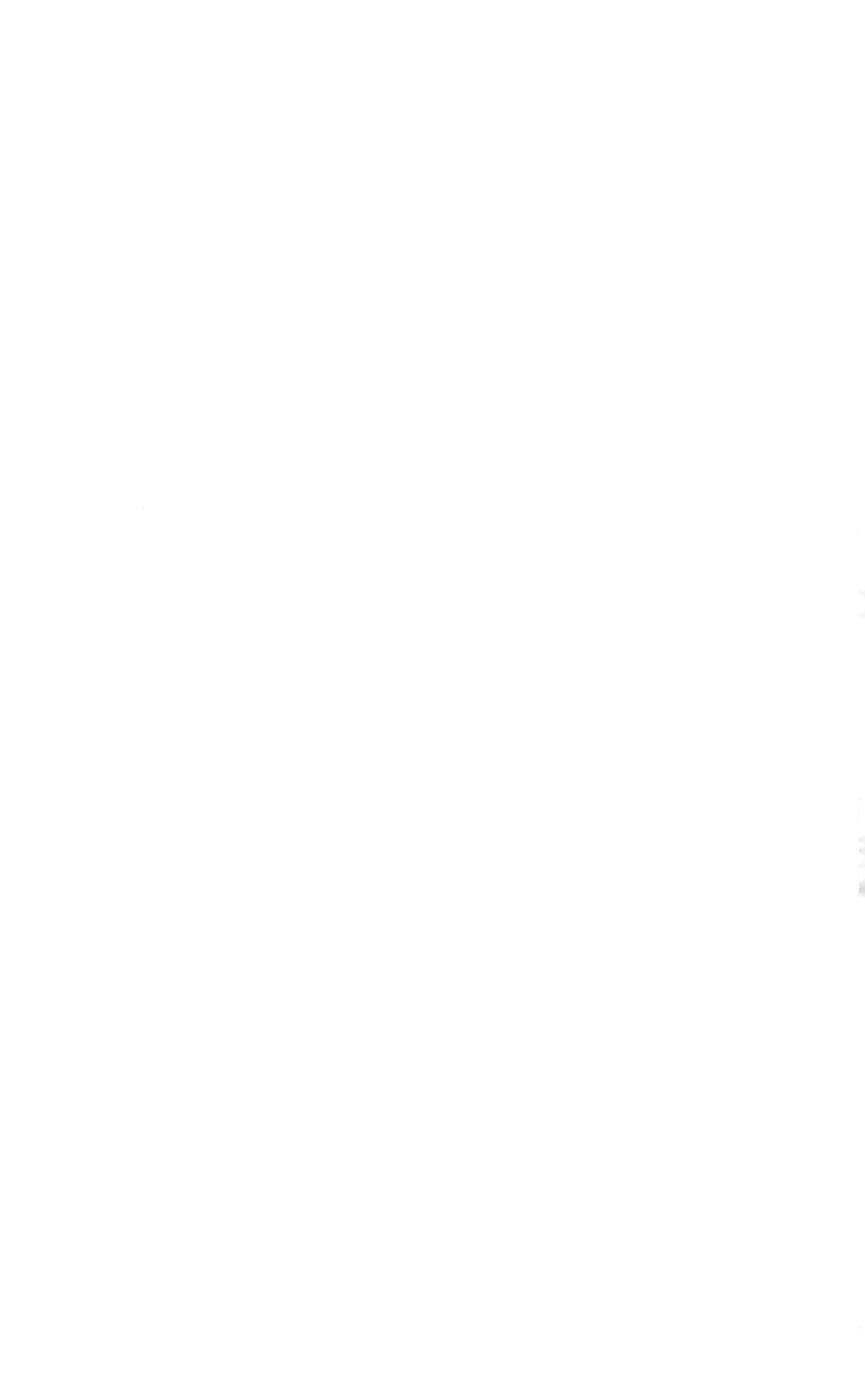

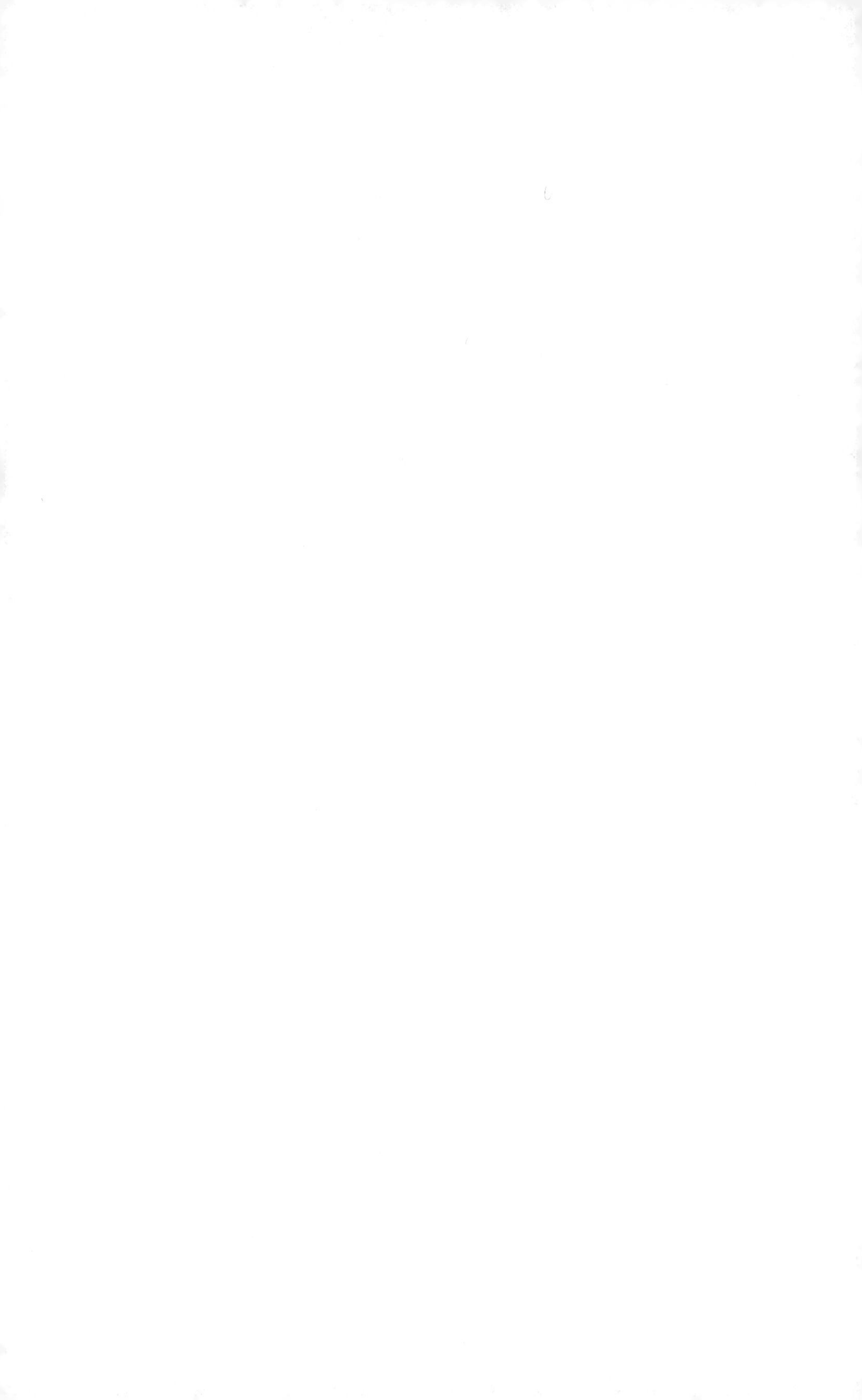

www.ingramcontent.com/pod-product-compliance
Lightning Source LLC
LaVergne TN
LVHW010545100826
845148LV00013B/2617

* 9 7 8 1 4 9 8 2 9 7 1 8 9 *